YOU KNOW YOU'VE BEEN IN JAPAN  TOO LONG...

Text and illustrations by
Bill Mutranowski

TUTTLE PUBLISHING
Boston • Rutland, Vermont • Tokyo

About the Bunny

Name: Stubby (Don't ask why).
Occupation: White space filler and, nominally, your guide to this book.
Personality: Recalcitrant and peevish, foil of every icky-sweet, cutesy character that ever romped across the Japanese landscape. Tends to see the world in terms of pink and white.
Likes: Speaking his walnut-sized mind.
Dislikes: Splitting hares.
Note: Want to know what Stubby thinks about Japan? To find out, watch him in the corner as you flip the pages of this book from left to right.

ウサギのプロフィール
名前：スタビィ。
職業：単なる本の余白埋め係。一応、この本の案内人。
性格：怒りっぽくてあまのじゃく。日本のかわいい人気キャラクター達をつい引き立ててしまう。
なんでも白黒つけたがる（でもうさぎだから白ピンクつけたがる）。
好きなこと：大したことない意見を言うこと。
嫌いなこと：細かいことをごちゃごちゃ言われること。
注意点：スタビィは日本についてどう思っているのか知りたい？もし、知りたかったらこの本の右下の彼
のことを見ながら左から右へパラパラめくってください。

Published by Tuttle Publishing,
an imprint of Periplus Editions

Copyright © 2003 Tuttle Publishing.
Rabbit character © 2003 Bill Mutranowski
All rights reserved.

First Tuttle edition, 2003
ISBN 0-8048-3380-X

Printed in Singapore
08 07 06 05 04   10 9 8 7 6 5 4 3 2

Distributed by:

Japan: Tuttle Publishing
Yaekari Building, 3F, 5-4-12 Osaki, Shinagawa-ku. Tokyo 141-0032
Tel: (03) 5437 0171 Fax: (03) 5437 0755 Email: tuttle-sales@gol.com

North America, Latin America & Europe: Tuttle Publishing
Airport Industrial Park, 364 Innovation Drive, North Clarendon, VT 05759-9436
Tel: (802) 773 8930 Fax: (802) 773 6993 Email: info@tuttlepublishing.com

Asia Pacific: Berkeley Books Pte Ltd
130 Joo Seng Road, #06-01/03, Singapore 368357
Tel: (65) 6280 1330 Fax: (65) 6280 6290 Email: inquiries@periplus.com.sg

Foreword

Anyone who spends even a little time in Japan will have a few good stories to tell when they get back home. But rubbing elbows with the Japanese, on their own turf, is good for more than just a laugh. The experience can give you a lot of insight into yourself. And that's not the kind of thing you can pick up in any old souvenir shop.

This book is for anyone who can read English (and even if you can't, you can always look at the pictures) and especially for those who already know a little something about Japan (I guarantee that it will confuse you even more). But it is dedicated to all those trailblazing expatriates who have been crazy enough to actually try and live alongside the natives in this very (insert favorite stereotype here) country.

I like to think that the mere presence of we foreigners in their Montana-sized enclave is a spur to Japan's own efforts to "internationalize". That's a holy grail of an objective that the Japanese seem hellbent on realizing. Problem is, they haven't yet defined for themselves what it means. But they'll figure it out someday. And when they do, with luck, they'll realize that they have more in common with the rest of the world, i.e., *gaijin*, than not.

　金髪外人の青い目に映った日本へようこそ。私は日本に15年も住んでいますから、皆さんの中学生のお子さんより在日歴が長いことになります。しかしながら、私が日本人に馴染んでいるのと同じようには、皆さんは私に馴染んでいないようです。とりわけ、外人だと思われているからこそ、私はこの本が書けたのでしょうね。そんな意味では、僕をヨソモノ扱いしていただいて、皆様に感謝、感謝！

　この本を書いた目的は、「有名になって、印税をもらって左うちわで暮らす」ということ。それから、他の国に住んでいる60億以上（世界人口の98％）の人々に、日本に少しばかりの興味を持ってもらおうと考えたのです。そう、これは誰かがやらなくてはいけないことです。私たちは世界中とのコミュニケーションが瞬時にとれる時代に生きているのに、未だに日本についての固定観念が拭いきれません。外国での日本人のイメージといえば、お茶をすすりながら折り紙をしている芸者とか、組織の歯車—働きバチ会社員……。こんなステレオタイプを作り出してしまった理由は、単に「外国人が無知だから」だとは言えません。自分たちを理解してもらおうという日本人の働きかけも足りないのです。

　本当の日本の姿、それは寺や着物やサムライだけではありません。ラブホテルにグッチのバック、それから（嬉しいかな、悲しいかな）ガイジンも真の日本の一部です。そんなガイジンの一人として、日本の読者の皆様にちょっと辛口な本書を少しでも楽しんでいただけたらと願っています。伝統的な火祭り（どんど焼きとか）で、この本を燃やして下さってもそれはそれで嬉しいのです……。何はさておき、今この本を立ち読みしているあなた、すぐそこのレジできちんと買ってくださいね。

あなたは「いくつのご家庭をお持ちですか？」と聞く

Having a little trouble pronouncing those Rs and Ls? Is your speech devoid of idioms, slang and words longer than five letters? Are you losing it linguistically? Well, you could find an English conversation teacher and take a little refresher course. What's that you say? You are an English conversation teacher?

最近RとLの発音が下手になったね。慣用語句やスラング、それにアルファベット五つ以上の単語が口から出て来ないなんて事はない？ それって、英語を忘れている証拠だよ。先生を探して英会話をブラッシュアップしたらどう。え？ 君自身が英語を教えているんだっけ。

4分半待ってられないから、満員電車に詰め込まれる

Ahh…laid back, mellow, stop-and-smell-the-roses of Tokyo. In your dreams! Not only is it one of the most densely populated cities on Earth, people there always seem to be in a hurry and busy with something or other. The pace slows down a bit on weekends, though—when the trains come 6 minutes, 17 seconds apart.

落ち着いてくつろげる、ゆったりとした時間が流れる東京。まさか！ この世界で指折りのすし詰め都市では、そんなことあるわけない。何しろみんなあくせくしてせわしないんだから。でも、週末は様子が全然ちがうかも。電車の間隔が6分17秒もあるよ。

少しでも体を動かす時に「ヨイショ」と言う

Ittai is Japanese for "ouch," and *otto* translates as "oops." But how to say *yoisho* in English? In the U.S.A., where obesity is practically the national pastime, it would have to be something like "grunt," immediately followed by "groan...creak...pop" and finally, "call 911!"

「痛い！」も「おっと！」も英語で言えるけど、「よいしょ」は何だっけ？ アメリカは肥満天国だから、こんな感じになるのかなぁ。まず、「ウウッ」と言って「ウウーン」とうなって、次は「ウグー」に「ポキッ！」で、最後は「救急車を呼べ」ってことに。

できるだけ他人に迷惑を掛けないようにストライキをする

Strikes, pickets and other such public demonstrations are pretty rare in Japan. It's not that everybody's happy about the way things are; they just think confrontation is something to be avoided. You know, the group harmony thing. It adds ups to a stable, well-ordered and politically inert society. So go ahead and have your sit-in. Just don't expect anyone to join you.

ストライキやデモなんて、日本ではほとんど見かけないね。だからといって、みんなが今のままでいいと思っているわけじゃない。ただ、日本人はなるべく衝突をさけたいだけ。そして集団の和こそが一番というわけ。その結果、社会は安定して秩序があると同時にマンネリ。え？ 君、デモがしたいのか？ やってみたら。誰もいっしょにやってくれなくてもよければね。

意味のない英語のフレーズがついている洋服をかっこいいと思ってしまう

Native English-speaking newcomers to Japan can get in a tizzy about how their mother tongue is twisted beyond recognition. There are cryptic English song lyrics, meaningless English ad slogans, hilarious English signs and incomprehensible English instructional manuals. But you've gotta admit that anything makes more sense than *nihon-go*.

日本に来たばかりの英語圏の外人はむかついてる。それは日本人のめちゃくちゃな英語の使い方のせいさ。意味不明の歌詞やわけの分からない広告コピー。笑っちゃう看板にチンプンカンプンの使用説明書。英語とは思えない。でも、ニホンゴを理解するよりましかぁ。

一本の木と一つのベンチ、少しばかりの土があれば、そこが公園だと思う

Nature in Japan is great, if you can find some. That's not to say it doesn't exist. You'll just have to put some distance between yourself and the densely populated mega-cities of Tokyo and Osaka first. Meanwhile, don't expect to frolic barefoot through the grass at a nearby park during your lunch break. But you can always park yourself in the shade of a vending machine.

日本の自然はすばらしい。もし、見つけられたらの話だけど。自然がないって言ってるわけじゃないよ。ただ、東京や大阪みたいなところから離れない限りは森林なんてない。だから、昼休みに近くの公園で芝生の上を裸足で飛び跳ねるなんて期待できない。自動販売機の日陰で一休み、なんてことならいつだってできるけど。

死に物狂いでエスカレーターまで走るのに、乗ったらただ立ってるだけ

The pace in Japan can be downright frenetic. But those escalators are like speed bumps. Curious, the way some people just stand there, when mere moments before they were meteors hurtling through space. But hey, go with the flow. So you'll be a little late for your aerobics class. It's better than the stairs, right?

日本人の歩くペースはイカレてる。エスカレーターまでは宇宙から飛んでくる隕石みたいにすっ飛んでいくのに、乗った途端じっと立っているなんて変だよ。それでも、皆と同じようにしていいよ。そのせいでエアロビクス・ダンス教室にちょっと遅れるけど、階段使うよりいいんでしょ？

「すみません」と、いつ言われたのか思い出せない

That remarkable Japanese courtesy isn't always all it's cracked up to be. Maybe it's the survival instinct that turns some people into human bowling balls. Suffice it to say the natives don't always look where they're going, or care where you're going. Like that little old lady. You'd think she'd know better. But try not to take it personally. After all, you're not the first person she's bowled over today.

日本人は礼儀正しさで有名だけど、あてにならないって感じ。サバイバルの本能がそうさせるのか、人間ボウリングボールになってしまう人もいる。他人がどこへ向かうのか見てないし、気に掛けてない。おばあさんまでマナーが悪いんだ。お年寄りっていうものは礼儀にうるさいはずなのに。あまり気にしない方がいいよ。彼女のスコアに貢献したピンは君だけじゃないからね。

箸でセイウチの真似をすることをしなくなった

Chopstick etiquette dictates that these implements be used only for stuffing food into your own trap. No drumming on the table, or trying to catch that pesky fly or stabbing at the air to make your point. And most important, you mustn't wander into your fellow diner's territory. But hotchpotch is an exception. For this meal you may dip your sticks right in, along with everyone else, which may seem a little contradictory to fastidious types.

箸は食べ物を自分の口に運ぶ時だけ使うのがエチケットだよ。だからテーブルをバンバン叩いたり、うるさいハエを捕まえたり、箸を使って物を指し示したりするものじゃないんだ。でも一番行儀が悪いのは、他人の皿に箸をつっこむこと。と、いっても鍋の時は例外。口に入れた箸をみんなが一つの鍋に入れてもいいんだ。潔癖症の外人には、ちょっと理解しがたいけどね。

「しょうがない」を口にするだけではなくて、心からそう思う

Throughout its history, Japan has been ravaged by earthquakes, floods and Godzilla. So maybe it's disaster and calamity that have instilled in the natives a sense of resignation about things beyond human control, and inspired the well-worn "It can't be helped." Problem is, in modern times, "it" often can be helped. So *Shou ga nai* may also serve as just so many weasel words.

日本では地震、洪水、さらにゴジラまで天災の歴史があるでしょ。だから人間の力ではどうすることも出来ないという諦めの気持ちが、日本人に植えつけられたのかもね。「しょうがない」はこんなふうに生まれた言葉。でもさぁ、科学の進歩した現代なら「しょうがある」ことも多いじゃない？ なのに何もしない逃げ道として「しょうがない」とまだ言い続けてるんだ。

花粉症の季節になったら、日本人と同じようにマスクをしてもいいと思ってしまう

A lone *gaijin*. In a convenience store. Wearing a mask. Can you blame the clerks for being uneasy? They read the newspapers, which are filled with reports of *gaijin* crime. Unfortunately, misinformation and half-truths masquerading as facts abound. Which can make it tough for a guy who only wanted a Snickers bar.

連れもなく、マスクをかけてコンビニにいったなら、店員がオロオロするのは当然でしょ。だって新聞に外人犯罪の記事がいっぱい載っているんだから。問題はそれらしい嘘やガセネタがたくさんあるってことなんだ。君はただ、チョコを買いに来ただけなのに。外人はつらいよ。

You Know You've Been in **VAPAN** -Too-Long-When...

YOU LIKE TO EAT YOUR WHALE AFTER WATCHING IT.

ホエール・ウォッチングの後、鯨料理を食べる

"Free Willy"–style sentimentality about our orca friends is unusual in Japan. Maybe that's why so little domestic ire is raised when whale-hungry hunters and pols call for more harpooning of these creatures. In fact, Grandma may want a Minke, but younger people are indifferent. Now, if they were to Kentucky-fry it…

映画『フリーウィリー』で見るような、シャチを友達として愛する日本人はあまりいない。だから捕鯨復活論にあまり反対の声が上がらないんじゃない？ 実際、おばあさんは、クジラの味が懐かしいかもしれないけど、若い人には食べ物という意識なし。「ケンタッキー・フライド・クジラ」になったら大人気かもしれないけど。

You Know You've Been in VAPAN (%@!!) Too Long When...

YOU NEVER HUG GUYS (EXCEPT WHEN YOU'RE DRUNK, WHICH IS OFTEN).

酔ってしまえば、男同士でも抱き合う（飲みに行くのはしょっちゅうだけど）

Touchy-feely is not a term that one ordinarily associates with Japanese men. And Japanese decorum dictates more personal space than in, say, North America (enough to bow without knocking heads?). But all bets are off when you're soused, because the usual rules are suspended. Maybe that's why some natives jokingly refer to their own country as a drunkard's paradise. *Gaijin* take note: booze may excuse some kinds of socially deviant behavior, like public hugging.

日本のオヤジたちはベタベタしない。たしかに北アメリカよりも人と距離を置くのが日本の礼儀なんだけど。（おじぎをする時に頭がぶつからないくらいかな？）でも酒の席ではそんなことはおかまいなし。いつもの約束事はちょっと置いておく。この国は酔っ払い天国だから、人前で男同士が抱き合うなんてあやしい行動もゆるされるんだ。

You Know You've Been in **VAPAN** Too Long When...

YOU SPONTANEOUSLY WHISTLE THE GARBAGE TRUCK SONG.

ゴミ収集車の流すメロディーを口笛で吹く

Unless you've checked in to a mountaintop buddhist monastery, to live almost anywhere in Japan is to be constantly subjected to noise: beeping cell phones, blaring train station announcements, supermarket jingles that repeat incessantly, whining motorcycles, stressed out dogs. Phew! What you don't have to worry about is too much privacy.

山寺に出家でもしたなら別なんだけど、日本では朝から晩まで騒音づけ。携帯の着信音、駅のばかでかいアナウンス、スーパーでひっきりなしに流れる音楽、ヴィーン、ヴィーンとバイクの音、ストレスでギャンギャン吠え続ける犬。あーあ！日本ならプライバシーの侵害とやらで悩む必要なんて全然ないね。だって、はじめからそれは存在しないから。

32

写真を撮られる時におきまりのピースをポーズする

When and why Japanese young people began to raise two fingers and say "Peeeace" whenever their picture is taken is probably a mystery not worth solving. The word does stretch your mouth muscles into something resembling a smile. But you'd think they would utter something more directly related to the art of photography, like "cheese."

写真を撮る時に、若い人がVサインをして、「ピース！」と言うよね。それはいつから、どうして始まったんだろう。ま、どうでもいいことだけど。「ピース」と言うと、口のあたりが横に広がって笑顔に見えなくもないか。それより写真の専門用語に関係のあることを言った方がいいんじゃない。たとえば、「チーズ！」え？ 関係ないって？

自分の子供に「ブタはブーブーとなくよ」と教える

Try these on for size: a dog says *wan-wan*, a frog says *kero-kero*, and a duck says *gaa-gaa*. Other Japanese words for sounds almost make sense—a pencil rolling across a tabletop is *koro-koro*. And by the way, *pika-pika* means to flash brilliantly and *chu-chu* is a mouse squeaking. Put them together and you've got *Pika Chu*. Now, isn't that a lot easier to remember than "onomatopoeia"?

ちょっとためしにやってみようか。犬は「ワンワン」、カエルは「ケロケロ」、アヒルは「ガアガア」。他にも音に関しては変だなと思うけど、テーブルの上を鉛筆が「コロコロ」転がるなんてのは、まあね。ところで「ピカピカ」はパッと光ることだし、「チューチュー」はねずみの鳴く声。この二つをいっしょにすると「ピカチュー」になるというわけ。ね、外人の君には onomatopoeia（訳：擬声語・擬態語）という難しい英単語より覚えやすいと思わない？

You Know You've Been in
VAPAN なの!! Too Long When...

YOUR NEW FAVORITE "SINGER" SINGS LIKE A HINGE.

ひどく音痴のシンガーが最近のお気に入りだ

She's got it all: a cute face, charm, sex appeal, the perfect outfit and makeup. Everything, that is, except a pair of vocal chords. You'd be surprised at how many Japanese pop stars can barely carry a tune. But the natives don't seem to mind because, as much as anything, it's appearance and style that enthrall them. So all aboard! Next career stop, the TV drama.

彼女にはシンガーとしての素質がある。かわいくて、ちょっとセクシーで、ファッションもメークもきまってる。でも、肝心の声がね……。まぁ、信じられないくらい音痴の歌手がたくさんいるよ。ルックスとカリスマ性があれば、日本人はそんなこと構わないんだ。歌手で人気がでれば、次はテレビドラマに出演するはずさ。

雨の日にスーパーの入り口で、必ず新しい傘用の「コンドーム」をつける

Umbrella condoms epitomize the Japanese love of cleanliness and convenience. But you'll notice that virtually everyone grabs a fresh one, even though the disgarded ones are only as dirty as the rain that fell on someone else's umbrella! What gives? Well, you wouldn't reuse the other kind of condom, now would you?

日本人にとって清潔さと便利さがなによりだっていうのは、傘用「コンドーム」でよくわかるよ。みんなが新しいものを手にとる。なぜ？　だって、一回使ったコンドームには傘の汚れしかついていないのに。その雨は自分の傘についたものと同じでしょ。一体何を考えているのかなー？　コンドームというものは使い捨てと思いこんでいるから？

40

12月24日の夜にはクリスマスの飾りを片付ける

Christmas in Japan is inspired by the film *Home Alone*, not the Bible (unless you are among the one percent of the population who is Christian). So have some "Christmas cake" and set up that chintzy miniature tree. Then just pack it up before you go to bed (after all, tomorrow is just another day). And your outdoor lights? They make your house look like a Beverly Hills mansion, so they can stay up a bit longer.

日本人にクリスマスを祝う気持ちにさせているのは、聖書じゃなくて、映画『ホーム・アローン』だよ（人口の１％いるクリスチャンを除いて）。クリスマスケーキを食べ、ちゃちな作り物のツリーを飾る。それを24日の夜にはもう片付けちゃう。夜なのに屋外のイルミネーションもしまうのかって？ そんなわけないでしょ。まるでビバリーヒルズの家みたいに見えるから、しばらくそのままだよ。

You Know You've Been in JAPAN Too-Long-When...

YOU MOONLIGHT AS A MINISTER, EVEN THOUGH YOU'RE AN ATHEIST.

神様なんていないと信じているのに、牧師のバイトをする

In Japan, form often supersedes substance, and attitudes toward religion are…well, flexible. Witness the wild popularity of church weddings in a society where only one percent of the population is Christian. So if you're a *gaijin* who looks the part, you may be hired to perform the ceremony. After all, in Japan "the play's the thing" and appearances count for a lot. Not a Christian? No sweat—neither are the bride and groom!

日本では、中身より体裁という場合が多いみたい。そして、宗教に対して日本人は……まぁ、うるさくない。だって、キリスト教の信者は１％しかいないのに、チャペルウェディングはみんなの憧れ。だから、牧師っぽい外人なら、結婚式場の職にありつけるよ。結局日本では、「らしさ」と「かたち」に左右される。え？君、クリスチャンじゃない？ ヘーキヘーキ。花嫁、花婿も同じだからね。

みんなが通るドアを自分もどうしても使いたくなる

In Japan, people are used to having things decided for them by all manner of higher ups: teachers, doctors, bosses, mothers-in-law. Independent thought isn't exactly the order of the day. So when word from above is lacking or unclear, people tend to follow the crowd. Or just dawdle and wait for a sign. Lord, show me a sign!

日本人は自分のことを目上の人に決めてもらうことを当然と思っている。教師、医者、上司、義理ママのいいなり。誰かに頼らなきゃ生きていけない。だから上からの指示がないとみんなして同じ行動に走るか、指示があるまでオロオロと待ってる。「神よ、私に指令をお与えください！」

本物の芸者を見たことがある

A visitor to Japan from Canada, for example, is more likely to run into a fellow Canadian before she runs into a *geisha*. Samurai are even rarer. But if you've got your heart set on catching a glimpse of one of these high-class entertainers, you'll want to head for Kyoto. Your other option is to build a time machine and transport yourself back to, say, 1920.

カナダの観光客が同じカナダ人に出くわすよりも、芸者を見かける方がまれだよね。侍を見るなんてマジで無理。それでも、かの高級エンターテイナーの姿を一目でも拝みたいなら、京都へ行くか、タイムマシーンで1920年代に戻るしかないね。

外人の友達に「本当だよ！ラーメン博物館にはまっちゃったよ」という

Yet another manifestation of the Japanese obsession with food. You wouldn't think a society would get all that excited over a bowl of noodles, but expertly prepared ramen is practically a delicacy. And hole-in-the-wall ramen shops, a favorite setting for television dramas, inspire warm, cozy feelings and nostalgia. The occasional cockroach and all.

これも日本人の食べ物に対する思い入れのひとつ。どんぶり1杯のラーメンになぜこんなにも社会全体が夢中になれるの？信じられない。その味に特別なこだわりがあるラーメンはキャビアに負けないくらい。テレビドラマなんかによく登場する狭くて汚いラーメン屋は、なぜか懐かしくて温かい気持ちになる。時たま見かけるゴキブリにすらね。

年に2回くらい子供と向き合う時間を過ごす

The company is the center of your typical salaryman's life. Long hours and grueling commutes mean that, for purposes of child rearing, a lot of families are de facto one-parent units. So well-intentioned Dad may not be very practiced at connecting with the kids when he does get some time off. Here's an idea, Pop: if the kiddies aren't interested in washing the car with you, there's always that modern facilitator of familial bonding—the video game.

普通のサラリーマンにとって、会社は生活の中心。お父さんたちが、会社勤めでへとへとになっているから、子育てはお母さん任せ。多くの家庭が母子家庭みたい。たまに休みがとれた時、お父さんは子供と向き合う気持ちがあっても、どうすればいいか分からない。ね、ね、お父さん。もしお子さんが洗車の手伝いを嫌がっても心配いりませんよ。親子をつないでくれる最新の強い味方テレビゲームがあるじゃない？

52

本音と建前の見分けがつく

Situations, rather than absolute principles, tend to dictate your course of action in Japan. Likewise, natives think in terms of heartfelt sentiments and those you merely display to others. Sometimes they're the same, sometimes not. Your mission, Jim, should you decide to accept it: try and tell the difference.

日本では、筋を通すことよりむしろ、その場その場でやり過ごすことが多い。その上、日本人は相手にみせる本音と建前を区別する。その時によって両方が同じこともあるけど、違うこともある。『ミッション・インポシブル』みたいに「ジム、君がこの作戦を引き受けるとすれば、この二つの違いをいってみろ。」

天皇制についての議論を耳にすると、とても不愉快になる

In Japan, you'll neither see paparazzi photos of nor hear critical public commentaries about the emperor, his wife, his family, his relatives, his friends or the guy who shines his shoes. That's because the topic is taboo. Period. No ifs, ands or buts. Well, maybe a few buts, but you'll definitely want to keep your voice down.

日本でパパラッチの皇室スクープ写真なんてお目にかかれないし、皇室に批判的な話は耳にしないでしょ。天皇、皇后、皇族にはじまって、その友人たちや皇室付きの靴磨きのオッサンまでもタブーの対象。絶対ダメ！「もしも」とか「だって」とかもありえない。それでも「けれど」と言いたいなら、声をひそめなくちゃダメだよ。

ゴージャスな結婚式を挙げたいので、ホテルのロビーでする

And you thought hotels were for **after** the wedding. Look at it this way. The church was booked. And you've got guests coming in from out of town who will need a place to stay. And you want to make a big, Western-style impression. It's also a money-making opportunity for the hotel. So everybody wins! Just don't start your honeymoon in the lobby.

外人の君は今までホテルって結婚式の後に行くものと思ってたでしょ。何故こんな場所を選んだかというと……なんせ教会は予約でいっぱいだし、泊まりがけでくる招待客がいる。それに盛大でヨーロピアンムードたっぷりにしたいからでしょ。ホテル側だっていい商売になる。双方いい事ずくめだよね。でも、ハネムーンまでホテルのロビーでするっていうのは、いくらなんでもやり過ぎじゃない？

58

日本アカデミー賞を受賞した人の名前を全部言える

Gaijin are by definition strange. But if you prefer Japanese films to, say, Hollywood fare, you might qualify as a *henna gaijin*, i.e., a Japanese wannabe. Paradoxically, among real Japanese, American movies tend to be much more popular than the domestic kind. So if you really want to go native, see the next Harry Potter sequel. Got it?

君がハリウッド映画より日本の映画が好きなら、「へんな外人」ということになる。いわゆる日本かぶれってやつだ。逆に日本人の間では邦画よりアメリカ映画の方がずっと人気がある。だから君が本物の日本人になりたいなら、次回は「ハリー・ポッター」の続編を見なくちゃ。オーケー？

60

参加者は外人だけなのに「乾杯」を待つ

Why be relaxed and casual when you can be uptight and formal? You're in Japan now, so leave your spontaneity at the door and follow party protocol. That means raising your glass simultaneously with **everyone** in attendance. No maverick celebrating. After the *kampai* you'll also want to be sure to clink glasses with as many other guests as is humanly possible before imbibing.

そんなにリラックスしてないで、もっと緊張して真面目にやって。日本のパーティーではそうしなきゃ。ドアのところに自分らしさを置いてパーティーの掟にしたがって過ごすんだ。つまり一瞬でも狂わずに、他のみんなと同時にグラスを上げろってこと。一人で勝手にお祝い気分になっちゃダメだよ。乾杯の次は必ず無理やりにでも、なるべく多くの人とグラスを鳴らさなきゃ飲めないよ。

「外人」と呼ばれることはもう平気

Some *gaijin* never get used to that label. Maybe it's because the natives won't let them forget it. Fact is, as long as you're in Japan you'll be an "outside person." But hey, don't blame your hosts if they make distinctions. After all, in modern times, foreigners have been going about their business in homogeneous *Nippon* for only about 150 years. And that's not enough time to get used to anything, is it?

外国人の中には「外人」と言われるのが、いつまでも気になる人もいる。それは日本人のオカゲサマです。実際のところ日本にいる限り、君は半永久的にヨソモノだ。でもほら、差別した日本人を責めないで。つまるところ欧米人が日本人だけの社会で生活しているのは、ここ150年くらいでしょ。何かに慣れるには150年は短いんだよ。

「礼金」を払うことは当然だと思う

Ah, the dreaded "key money." It is, in fact, a hefty cash gift forked over to a landlord simply for the privilege of paying him rent, a security deposit and, when the time comes, a lease renewal fee. This quasi-bribery, which seems to be rooted in an earlier time when demand for housing far outstripped supply, continues to piss off many a would-be foreign renter.

冗談じゃないよ、礼金を払うなんて！ 礼金は部屋を借りる権利、つまり家賃、敷金、更新料を払わせていただく権利ってやつを手に入れるために払うのさ。別名ワイロ。この習慣は、家の供給が需要に追いつかなかった昔の名残らしい。それが今も家を借りたい多くの外人にくやしい思いをさせている。

66

ちょっとそこの自動販売機まで妻のサンダルをつっかけて行く

The unwritten rule is this: if that errand will only take you down the street or around the corner, you're allowed to slip into whatever's near the door, without bothering with the laces. That's why the back of every single pair of shoes in Japan is mashed down flat as a pancake. So you see, there's nothing fetishistic about putting on the wife's mules once in a while. Unless you paint your toenails first.

お使いにちょっと通りに出るとか、そこの角までだったら、玄関にあるものを適当に履いて行っていい。誰の靴でもおかまいなしで、どんな靴でもサンダルみたいにつっかけて履く。そのせいで日本中の靴は、かかとがパンケーキみたいにペタンコ。そんなわけで、奥さんのミュールを履いても変態に見られない。でも足にペディキュアをしてたらヤバイかも。

後ろで掃除のおばさんが待っていても、平気で用が足せるようになった

It can be difficult enough to do your business in a public toilet, what with all of the other, er, activity going on. Now try concentrating with a female janitor who reminds you of your Aunt Gertrude hanging around. You could tell yourself that you're more conscious of her than she is of you, but who knows? And in case you were wondering, you won't find any male custodians in the ladies' room.

周りに人がいてリラックス出来ないから公衆トイレで用をすますのは大変だ。それに、自分のおばさん似の掃除婦がいれば、もっと緊張するよ。それほど彼女は僕のことを気に掛けていないと思えば楽なんだけど、はたしてどうかな？
ところで、女性用のトイレに掃除のおじさんはいないよね。なぜだ？

心を癒したい時に、アイスクリームじゃなくて目玉や吸盤がついているものを楽しむ

You could pig out on Haagen Daz (which is widely available). But as long as you're in an exotic country, why not take a walk on the wild side when you're feeling blue? In Japan you can console yourself with all kinds of lower forms of animal life. They're less fattening than ice cream. And who knows—while you're munching away you may even meet a pair of sympathetic eyes.

日本にだってハーゲンダッツくらいある。でもせっかくこんなにエキゾチックな国にいるんだからさ、気分が滅入ってたら、ヤバイことに手を出してみないか？そんなときは、日本人がよく食べる下等動物の類なんかどう？ アイスクリームよりローカロリーだし。ムシャムシャやってる時に君は同情的な視線を感じるかも。

72

二回以上、能を見に行ったことがある

Many foreigners may find Noh, or traditional Japanese theater, about as riveting as watching water drain from a bathtub. Only it takes longer. Much longer. And truth be told, the natives aren't exactly climbing all over one another to get tickets, either. But it is something that every visitor to Japan should experience once. Or better yet, just say you did.

たくさんの外人にとって能とか伝統芸能を見ることは、お風呂のお湯が排水口に吸い込まれるのを見るのと同じくらいの面白さかな。ただ、それよりちょっと長いかな。いや、ずーっと長い。でも日本人だってチケット売り場に殺到しているわけじゃない。まぁせっかく日本に来たのなら見といて損はないけど、とりあえず「見たよ」と言っておこう。

あなたは愛情をこめて東京を「ビッグ・みかん」と呼ぶ

The Japanese aren't big on creative nicknames. Maybe that's because nicknames suggest informality, frivolity, and fun. And after all, we are talking about Japan here. So go ahead and think up a breezy moniker for your adopted Japanese hometown. But don't expect it to catch on.

例えばニューヨークをビッグ・アップルと呼ぶでしょ？ でも、日本人はそういう創造的なあだ名をあまりつけないよね。あだ名はくだけていて、馴れ馴れしく、ふざけている感じがするからかも。そういう雰囲気は日本社会と合わない。外人の君が日本のホームタウンにニックネームをつけたいの？ いいんじゃない。どんなにいい出来でも皆は使わないよ。

同じお笑い芸人がどの番組にも出ているのに、テレビは面白いと思う

Why is it that a handful of big-name talents tend to dominate the boob tube in Japan? Maybe the natives like the predictability. But it's hard to believe that they can't dig up at least a few more funny people among the 126 million or so inhabitants. Maybe they should tap into the Diet and its members. Some of those clowns are always good for a laugh.

なぜ日本では一握りのタレントがテレビを支配してるんだろう？　多分日本人はおヤクソクがおキニイリ。1億2千6百万の生息者からもっと面白い人を発掘出来ないなんて信じられないよ。国会議員なんてどうかな。あの能なしカボチャどもの中には、いつだっていい笑いのタネがあるからさ。

「海岸」といわれたら、あなたはコンクリートしか想像できない

Visitors to Japan may not be familiar with the bureaucratic behemoth that has, over the years, encased 60 percent of Japan's coastline in cement and lined the banks of all rivers and streams with concrete walls. Sure, some picture postcard vistas remain. But evidence of a "pave and build" mentality is everywhere. So just do what many of the natives do—grab that board and head to Hawaii!

日本では海岸の60%がセメントだらけ。どんな河川でも部分的にはコンクリートで固められている。この官僚のばかげた公共事業政策の証拠が都会にも田舎にも、あっちこっちにある。もう、絵葉書にあるような景色はほんの少しばかり。だから、サーフボードを手にハワイに行こう、日本人みたいに！

東京ディズニーランドに55回行ったのか、56回なのか分からない

There's just something about Disneyland, Mickey Mouse and his gang that seems to fit Japan like a glove. Maybe it's all that cuteness. Or maybe it's that everything about Disneyland is so...*genki*. For whatever reason, the Japanese can't get enough of old Walt's world. And given how fluent Mickey is in the local lingo, you might never guess that he's a *gaijin*.

不思議だけど、日本人はディズニーランド、ミッキーマウスやその仲間たちと相性がピッタリ。かわいいからかな？ それともディズニーランドは「元気」があふれているせいかも。なんだか分からないけど、日本人はディズニーランドにハマっている。まぁ、ミッキーの日本語がうますぎるから外人ということを忘れられちゃうんだね。

82

日本の総理大臣が、G8の他のリーダーと同じぐらい背があればいいなと思う

In the land of *wa*, you're a Japanese first and an individual second. So when you see one of your own out and about in the larger world doing great things, it's not, "Hey, that guy made good," but rather, "Hey, that Japanese guy made good." And all the better if he doesn't need elevator shoes—it'll reflect better on you.

「和」を尊ぶこの国では個人は二の次、まずは日本人である事が第一なんだ。海外で活躍している人を見ても「この人スゴイね」じゃなくて、「この日本人はすばらしい」となる。その人がシークレットブーツを履く必要がなければもっと誇らしい気分になれるんだけどね。

他の外人をじーっと見る

Gaijin stand out everywhere in Japan. They are just so...so **not** Japanese. And you can look forward to being stared at. A lot. The looks are neither hostile nor friendly. Most people probably just can't think of anything better to do. Of course, you could stare right back at the most grievous gawkers. But you'd better not—the Japanese consider it rude.

日本では外人はどこにいても目立つよね。だって、一目で日本人じゃないとわかるもの。ここにいると、じろじろ見られる楽しみを味わえるわけだ。まぁ、その視線には敵意があるわけじゃないけど好意もない。多分ほとんどの人が君を見る事より面白いことがないのかも。もちろん腹に据えかねるならにらみ返すことも出来るけど、それはしない方がいいよ。日本では、じっと見るのは失礼だから。

あなたはつい混血児を「ハーフ」、ゲイの人を「ホモ」と言ってしまう

In daily conversation the Japanese use lots of borrowed English. These loan words are adapted to Japanese sensibilities, so nuance may take a flying leap. In fact, you can often chuck the original meaning altogether. And PC? It's right over there on the desk.

日本人は日常会話で外来語をよく使う。でもそれは日本語感覚だから、もとの英語の意味と違っている。たとえば、向こうでハーフとホモは、差別的に受け取られてマズイよ。PCを知らないのかって？ あぁ日本人ならこう答えるだろうね、パソコンなら机の上にあるよって。このPCは差別用語を避けると言う意味なのに。

88

以前はコルベットだったけど、今はSuzuki Every Joy Pop Soundという車に乗っている

Sure there are sports cars in Japan. What you won't find are a lot of straight stretches of road where you can open up (70 percent of the country is mountains; the other 30 percent is people). So you settle for a functional set of wheels (albeit with a dashboard TV/navigation system), with a name that sounds like a brand of bubble gum. Yes, you've compromised. But you'll never lose "the look."

たしかに日本にもスポーツカーくらいある。でも宝の持ちぐされ。だって、ずっと続く直線道路なんてめったにお目にかかれない。（なにしろ国土の70％は山で、あとの30％が人間。）だから、風船ガムみたいな名前のついた、ただ走るだけの車で（カーナビくらいの装備はあるけど）我慢するしかない。まぁ、車がだめでも君はまだまだイケてるよ。

90

知り合いがいるのに気がついていない振りをする技をすっかりマスターした

There's a name for this—*shiranpuri*. I know that you know that I know you've noticed me. But let's pretend otherwise. Sometimes it's mutual, sometimes not. Either way, ignoring the other guy seems to be okay, if it spares you embarrassment or inconvenience. Of course, some *gaijin* may tell themselves "out of sight, out of mind." But in practice, the Japanese do it better. Much better.

その技は「知らんぷり」という。それは、相手を見て見ぬ振りをすること。時には二人とも、時には一方がそうする。べつに、どっちがしても構わない。何しろ日本人は恥ずかしがり屋だし、面倒くさいことは避けたい。むろん外人でも同じようなことをするけど、この道に関しては日本人のほうが何枚も上手だな。ずうっと。

鏡を見て、「俺の顔はなんて小さいんだろう！」と思ってしまう

Looks count for as much in Japan as anywhere. And if popular culture is any indication, the less Japanese and the more "Western" you look, the better. Double eyelids, dyed hair, and large breasts for women set a beauty standard that few can hope to match. So if your face tends toward narrow and well-defined, rather than round and flat, cheer up. You're one of the beautiful people!

日本でもルックスは大事だよね。最近はテレビや雑誌で二重まぶたに茶髪、大きなバストの西洋人ルックスが大人気。でも、それが似合う人はほとんどいないけどね。君が平べったい丸顔じゃなく、顔が小さくて彫りが深いなら、よろこんで。それだけで美男美女の仲間入りってわけだから。

94

先週末に豊年祭りを見物したことを本国の祖母に平気で話す

There are vaguely phallic tourist destinations, like the Leaning Tower of Pisa. And then there is the Tagata Fertility Festival, where a giant wooden dildo is paraded through the streets. If such risque reverie doesn't fit your image of Japan, don't worry—the Penis Festival is an anomaly in a country where the wonders of that particular organ are most commonly celebrated behind closed doors, at "love *hotels*."

あのさ、イタリアのピサの斜塔は少し男のあれに似ていない？ 同じような観光名物なら日本の豊年祭りだってどこにもまけていないよ。みこしの代わりに木製のでっかい男のシンボルを担いで、街を練り歩くんだから。何？ 君の日本のイメージに合わないって？ 気にしないで。こんな祭りは珍しいよ、つまりチン祭ってわけ。たいてい日本人は男のすばらしさを祝いたい時には、ラブホテルに行くほうがノーマルだからね。

必ず相手の男性にビールを注ぐ

Japan is a man's country in a man's world. Guys are usually first in the pecking order, and they take a certain amount of female subservience and deference for granted. Except maybe when in the company of Western women, who are perceived as "strong" and may be aware of the potential self-defense applications of an empty bottle of brew.

男中心の世界の中でも、日本は特に男の国だ。社会的な地位や立場は男が上で、女ってものは男に媚びを売って、何でもハイハイ言うのがいいと思われている。でも、欧米人の女性と一緒の時は様子が違うかも。日本人と違って彼女たちは「やる時はやる」オーラを発しているし、自分の権利を守る道具として、空のビールびんを想像できる知恵もあるからね。

普通預金の金利が0.002％に上がったら、すごく嬉しくなる

99

Which pays higher interest: a) a Japanese bank, or b) a mattress? If you have to do mental gymnastics before you can answer that, you know you're in Japan. Japanese people work hard and save a lot of their income. And their banks work equally hard at failing, being inefficient and not recovering bad loans made to crooked politicians and *yakuza* types. Oh, and the answer to the question is b.

A. 日本の銀行　B. たんす貯金　どっちが得するか？もしこの問題を真剣に考えなくちゃならないとしたら、それは君が日本にいる証拠だ。庶民は汗水流して働いてたくさんのお金を貯金する。一方、銀行はつぶれることに一生懸命。あのおたんこナスどもはむやみに金を貸し付けて、汚い政治家やヤクザに踏み倒されてもナスすべもない。ところで、さっきの答えはもちろん B。

どんな馬鹿が「船頭多くして船山に上る」ということわざを考えたのかな

The Japanese will go through pains to include everyone in the activities of the group. Everyone has to be involved, whether they're actually needed or not. That's why what might look to the casual observer like utter chaos is actually very highly organized chaos. Helpful hint: if the party's at your house, just hang loose; eventually someone will find you something to do.

全員で何かをする、というのが日本人のやり方。そんなに大人数でする必要がないような事でも、とにかくみんなでしなくちゃ気がすまない。だから、ただみんなでバタバタしているように見えるけど、ちゃんと物事はうまく運んでいる。そうだ、いい事を教えるよ。君の家でホームパーティーをするなら、気を使わなくていいよ。君の家なのに誰かが代わりにしきってくれるから

熱烈なカープファンだけれど、チームマスコットがアリクイにそっくりなことを
変だと思っていない

Like so much of what they borrow from abroad, the Japanese have reshaped American baseball in their own image. Check out the Chunichi Dragons logo—sure does look like the LA Dodgers' emblem. And long before the Tokyo Giants there were those other Giants in San Francisco. Well, at least some of their mascots are original. What's that you say? That anteater reminds you of the "Philadelphia Phanatic?"

日本人はよく海外のものをパクるよね。たとえばアメリカの野球。中日ドラゴンズのロゴはロスのドジャースにそっくり、東京ジャイアンツが生まれるずっと前にサンフランシスコにジャイアンツがあったよ。だけど少なくとも、チームマスコットは日本のオリジナルだね。待てよ。カープのへんなアリクイもどきは「フィラデルフィア・ファナティック」というやつに似てるんじゃない？

ただの風邪に四種類の薬を処方されて、とても満足だ

Cure, cure, cure—that's all these Japanese doctors seem to think about. Guess they're saving the prevention part for later. Anyway, if you're into medicinal drugs you've come to the right place. Physicians here tend to dispense them liberally. So have a seat. The doctor will be with you in…Oh, did we mention what the natives say?: "Wait three hours for a three-minute appointment."

治療、治療、治療しなきゃ。日本人の医者はそればっかり。予防の事は後で教えてくれるかな。薬飲まないと安心できないなら、日本は最高。日本の医者は気前よく薬を出すからね。だからお掛けになって。先生はすぐ来ますからね。おっと、いい忘れちゃった。「三時間も待ってたった三分の診察」は当たり前だよ。

イエスカノーを答える代わりに苦笑いをして困ったふりをする

When answering "yes" or "no" entails sticking your neck out even a little, the Japanese prefer vagueness. You don't want to step on any toes, or have an ill-considered promise boomerang and cause trouble for you. That's why you should just suck air. You also can communicate ambivalence (and cover your behind) with the extremely handy *Sou, desu ne*. Just make sure you say it with a straight face.

イエスかノーの選択って多少でもリスクがあるから、日本人は曖昧に答えたいんでしょ。誰かに迷惑になったり、断りきれないで後でマズイことになるのが嫌なんだよ。だから苦笑いでごまかす。さもなければ、「そうですねぇ……」という、チョー便利な逃げ道を使うんだよ。ただマジな顔して言わないとダメ。

女性の下着を見てとてもエッチな気分になる

It's not the sort of tidbit you'll read about in the tourist brochures. But judging from the late night TV, videos, and magazines they consume, more than a few Japanese men are fascinated by *panchira*, or catching a glimpse of a woman's underpants. And that's not all. In *Nippon* there's even a market for the used panties of high school-aged girls. What's so titillating about a piece of pubescent fabric? Hey, it's a (Japanese) guy thing.

これはガイドブックには載ってない情報だよ。日本人の男が見る深夜番組やエッチなビデオ、雑誌なんかみてると、結構みんなパンチラに興味があるみたい。つまり、女性の下着をちらっと見ること。それだけじゃないよ。もっと不思議なのは、日本で使用済みの女子高生のパンティが売買されてるんだ！なんで思春期の女の子の下着にそんなにそそられるんだ？いやほら、その謎の答えは日本人の男しか知らないのさ。

110

「ファンキーカレーエッグ、スパイシーポテト、ダブルマヨネーズ」ピザを外人のお客さんも好きだと思い込んでいる。

Were you thinking that the weirdest grub the Japanese could dish up was raw fish? Surprise! What they like to put on pizza will turn your head, and maybe your stomach, too. If, when your pizza arrives, it looks like the delivery person dropped it face down on the road along the way, don't panic. You've got the "Deluxe." So dig in!

日本の食べ物で一番変なものは刺身と思ってたかい？もっとすごいものがある。それは目が点になっちゃう、気持ち悪いピザのトッピングだよ。配達途中に中身をひっくり返しちゃったようなピザが届いてもパニックにならないで。それが、注文のデラックスピザだから。さぁ、どうぞ召し上がれ！

中身スカスカの豪華パッケージ入りクッキーを買っても、量をごまかされて
いると感じない（環境に悪いとも思わない）

Consumer rights advocacy and environmentalism are still rickshas in this Bullet Train society. Astronomically high prices are often taken for granted, product information is inadequate or falsified, and excessive packaging is the norm. So if you want to know exactly what's in those cookies and not end up with a mound of trash, you'll have to bake them yourself.

日本社会まるごとを新幹線とすれば、消費者の権利と環境についての意識は人力車並だ。なぜか。日本人は目玉が飛び出るようなばか高い値段を払うことになれている。そして商品の情報がでたらめだったり、足りなかったりする。しかも、余分なパッケージも多い。だから、山のようなゴミを出したくなくて、クッキーの材料をちゃんと知りたかったら、手作りにした方がいいよ。

You Know You've Been in JAPAN %@!! -Too-Long-When...

最近の主な政治的活動といえば、総理大臣の好物である自家製のキャベツの漬物についてのテレビ番組を見たことだけである

Democracy in Japan, such as it is, tends to be a top-down sort of thing. At the national level, the same corruption-prone fuddy duddies have been in power since the end of World War II. And among the docile public, respect for authority and the idea that you can't fight city hall have deep roots. Oh well, as long as the trains run on time…

民主主義って下の声が上にいくもんでしょ。でも日本では全く逆。戦後からワイロ漬けで石頭のオヤジたちが、相も変わらず権力の座に就いてるし、下々の者は権威を奉ってお上には逆らっちゃなんねぇ、って昔から思い込んでる。電車が時刻表通りに着く限り、まぁいいか。

あなたが読んでいる漫画を見て、プレーボーイの友達が赤面する

Graphic violence, rape, bloodshed. And if that shocks you, just wait till you see what's on the next page! The content of Japanese comic books seems to be debated by everyone but the Japanese themselves. Of course, many *manga* do address more wholesome subjects. But you won't be able to understand **them** just by looking at the pictures.

暴力やレイプ、流血。次のページはもっとひどいよ。日本の漫画は外人にあれこれ批判されているけど、当の日本人は問題にしてない。もちろん、中には健全なテーマを扱っているものもある。でもそんな複雑な内容を漫画の絵だけで理解するのは不可能だよ。

You Know You've Been in JAPAN Too Long When... %@!! KAWAIiii!

YOU HAVE BECOME ACUTELY AWARE OF CUTENESS (AND LET THE WORLD KNOW IT).

SALE

かわいい物に目がない

The Japanese are suckers for cuteness. Witness the mountains of yen they happily shell out for "character goods": notebooks, candy, clothing, toilet seat covers, anything featuring an image of the hottest (i.e., cutest) cartoon critter. Worse, there is a universal appeal to many of the lovable little munchkins the big name cute factories crank out. Which means *gaijin* may not be immune to their charms.

日本人はかわいい物を見ると高くてもつい手が出てしまう。ノート、キャンディ、洋服、トイレの便座カバーまで、今一番ホットなキャラクターのグッズなら手当たりしだいだ。日本の大会社がガンガン作ったかわいい動物キャラクターは、今や世界でひっぱりだこ。外人だって本家本元にやって来たら財布のひもがゆるくなるかもね。

Glossary

boo-boo: oink

chu-chu: squeak

gaa-gaa: quack

gaijin: a foreigner; literally an outside person

geisha: one of a class of traditional, professional female entertainers

genki: well, cheerful

half: a biracial person

henna gaijin: a gaijin who acts more Japanese than the Japanese themselves

homo: a homosexual

honne: one's true feelings

ittai: ouch

kampai: cheers

kawaii: cute

kero-kero: ribbit

koro-koro: the sound of, for example, a pencil rolling across a tabletop

love hotel: a class of hotels that cater to people seeking a place to have sex

manga: a comic book

mikan: a mandarin orange

nihongo: the Japanese language

Nippon: Japan

Noh: traditional theater

otto: oops

panchira: surreptitiously (or unintentionally) catching a glimpse of a woman's (or girl's) underpants

pika-pika: to flash brilliantly

reikin: "key money"; a cash gift paid to a landlord

shiranpuri: the act of ignoring someone you recognize, who may also recognize you

shou ga nai: It can't be helped

Sou desu ne…: Well, let me see…

tatemae: feelings one may merely display to others

wa: group harmony

wan-wan: bow-wow

yakuza: the Japanese mafia

yoisho: an utterance accompanying physical exertion

Acknowledgment

The author would like to thank, in order of appearance, the people of Japan, without whose Japaneseness this book about Japaneseness would not have been possible; the staff of Tuttle Publishing, Tokyo, for taking a second look at my proposal after it bounced off the rim of the wastepaper basket in their office during an impromptu game of makeshift basketball; Eric Oey, publisher, and Nancy Goh, production manager, and the staff of Periplus Publishing Group, Singapore, who gritted their teeth and saw the manuscript through, while also working on numerous other real books; and Hisae Tanaka and Sachiyo Takamizawa, whose diligence, attention to detail, and forbearance made the translation possible. I hope that someday they will return my calls.